A momento on your
visit to a Southern City

Laurence Decore, Mayor
July '84

EDMONTON

Pat Morrow
and
Carol Baker

EDMONTON

Pat Morrow
and
Carol Baker

Published by
WHITECAP BOOKS LTD.,
1615 VENABLES STREET,
VANCOUVER, B.C.
V5L 2H1

First Printing 1980
Copyright ® Whitecap Books Ltd.
ISBN 0-920620-17-5 (Paperback)
ISBN 0-920620-18-3 (Hardcover)
Printed in Canada

Credits

Design by
MICHAEL BURCH
Printed by
D.W. FRIESEN & SONS LTD.
ALTONA, MANITOBA
Colour separation by
NORTH WEST GRAPHICS LTD.
VANCOUVER, B.C.

The Photographers

The photography for this book was compiled by Pat Morrow, who also shot many of the photographs. Pat, a freelance photographer, is also involved in the sport of rock and mountain climbing. As well as 'Edmonton' Pat has photographed 'Calgary' and 'The Yukon' for other books in this series.

Additional photography is provided by J. A. Kraulis and Wilhelm Schmidt. J. A. Kraulis spends most of his time pursuing a very successful career in photography, and has had his material featured in several books. Wilhelm Schmidt is presently working as a commercial photographer and cinematographer. He has contributed work to various books, magazines, and documentary film programs about many areas and aspects of Canada.

The Writer

Carol Baker is a freelance travel writer, and has had her work published in many magazines and newspapers throughout North America. Carol has also written the books 'Calgary' and 'British Columbia: The Pacific Province'.

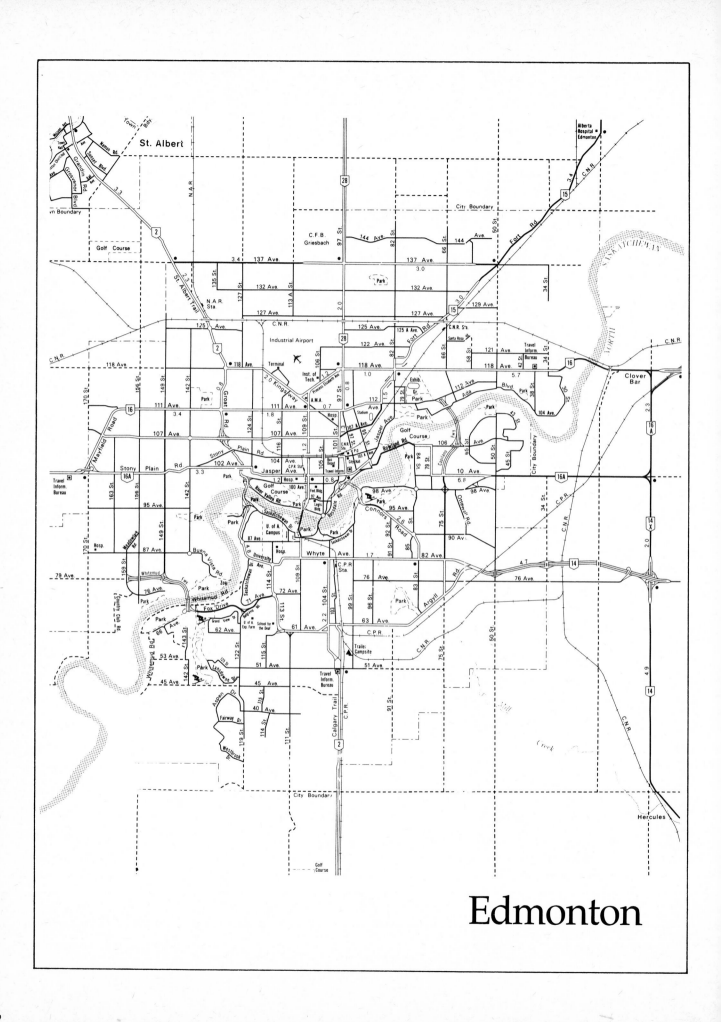

Edmonton

The City of Edmonton

Millions of years ago, geological forces in the area now known as Alberta stored away great pockets of oil and gas, and then covered them with layers of coal and clay. Glaciers advanced and retreated, leaving cold rivers, streams and lakes scattered across the vast northwestern plain. Rainfall and other climatic conditions rendered the soil rich, which gave birth to grass and boreal forests of spruce and poplar, creating a home for great numbers of birds and other animals.

Some 10,000 years ago, bands of native Indians roamed southward following the game. The fur-bearing animals furnished the Indians with skins for building shelters and for making warm clothes as well as with food, while the trees also provided shelter and fueled their campfires during the long, cold winter nights.

About two centuries ago, the first white men ventured into the western wilderness. Explorers like Anthony Henday, Alexander Mackenzie and David Thompson were seeking overland routes to the Pacific Ocean. Fur traders came looking for Indians who would exchange buffalo robes, the coveted pelts of otter and beaver, and pemmican for ostrich feathers, liquor, tobacco, guns, ammunition, axes and other tools.

In 1797 the North West Company built Fort Augustus, and the Hudson Bay Company built Fort Edmonton, probably named after a British estate belonging to the deputy-governor of the company. By the time the two companies merged in 1821, Fort Edmonton, located on the bank of the North Saskatchewan River, had become a major trading post. The man responsible for the fort's prosperity was the fur trader John Rowand, known as "Big Mountain" to the Indians.

The Fort housed about 130 Europeans who spent their days trading furs and cultivating crops of barley, oats and potatoes. Indians were contracted to bring in buffalo meat and fish, and timber was rafted downstream for firewood and for building boats.

In the 1850's, Methodist missionaries and Father Lacombe and his Grey Nuns arrived to bring spiritual riches to the western whites, Métis and Indians. Meanwhile, prospectors were coming to the Edmonton area seeking more tangible wealth in the form of gold dust along the North Saskatchewan River. They found little.

After the Riel Rebellion ended in 1885, there was relative peace in the region, although by this time about half the Indian population had died from smallpox. More settlers and a few whiskey traders were moving northward. Sturdy York boats were plying the rivers to and from Winnipeg. Cattle and wheat fields were replacing furs and buffalo. The North West Mounted Police set up a fort, and Donald Ross built Edmonton's first hotel. Peter Pond confirmed Alexander MacKenzie's discovery of the bituminous sands, and Indians patched their canoes with tar from the same oil sands which today are producing large quantities of synthetic oil.

By the time Edmonton was incorporated as a town in 1892, it boasted 700 citizens, a newspaper, a school, telegraph service, and a railway route to Calgary.

Then, in 1898, news of the Yukon gold find filtered south, and hordes of fortune hunters streamed north from all over the continent. Edmonton flourished as a commercial centre, supplying miners with food and equipment for the arduous trek to the Klondike gold fields. But many would-be miners gave up their quest and returned to Edmonton to settle.

When Alberta became a province in 1905, Edmonton, which had become a city the year before, was named the capital city. At this time, most of its 1,800 citizens were young men, although a few hardy women had accompanied their husbands here. The motive power was oxen and horses. Percherons and Clydesdales transported loads of lumber and hay through the dirt streets, while strings of pack horses moved in and out of the city. Smart surreys taxied more prosperous Edmontonians across the city.

In 1912, the Legislative Building was built, in Victorian-style architecture with its vaulted dome, on the site of the original Fort Edmonton. It still sits gracefully in the heart of town overlooking the North Saskatchewan River valley.

The motor car reached Edmonton and homesteaders kept on coming. The airplane arrived in the 1930s, when bush pilots like Punch Dickens, Max Ward, and Grant Mc-

Conachie flew in and out of Blatchford Field, now the Industrial Airport, helping to establish the city as a trade and transportation centre.

It was the discovery of oil at Leduc, 30 kilometres south, in 1947 which secured Edmonton's prosperity. Since that time the city has experienced tremendous growth and is now home for more than half a million people. Alberta, whose present population is approaching the two million mark, is almost synonymous with expansion and prosperity. The strong westward shift in population and economic power has bolstered Edmonton's market position.

A young, educated population, forestry reserves to the north in the Peace River district and to the west, and productive farmland have helped lead the city to prosperity. Agriculture, based on renewable resources, is Alberta's original prime industry. And in recent years a multitude of service industries have flourished.

But it is oil, often referred to as black gold, which fuels the economy. The city is the geographic centre of the oil and gas industry in Alberta. More than 80 percent of the producing wells in the province are located in the Edmonton marketing area. The Alberta Oil Sands, 440 kilometres north, contain an estimated 330 billion recoverable barrels of oil, equivalent to more than half the total world conventional reserves of oil. Edmonton refineries currently produce 60 percent of Canada's petroleum products. East of the city lies "Refinery Row", a string of industrial chemical plants, gigantic storage tanks, and pipeline pumping stations. Several multimillion dollar petrochemical complexes, currently under construction, will produce building-block materials for the plastics industry on a global scale. Thermal coal production is expected to reach 30 million tons by 1983, and gas reserves are also significant.

This new prosperity is bringing modern-day settlers to the city at the present rate of about 2,000 a month. An added attraction is the fact that Alberta has no sales tax, and property and income taxes are the lowest in the country. The province of Alberta boasts the richest non-national government in the western world. The $6 billion Heritage Fund, a trust fund set up by the province to provide for continuing economic viability when the oil runs out, obtains its revenues from taxes levied on the petroleum industry.

The 1980 "Homecoming", a commemoration of Alberta's 75 years as a province, is heralded as the greatest celebration in the history of the province. As provincial capital, Edmonton, which hosts about three million visitors each year, is the focal point of the festivities.

The highlight of the year is Klondike Days, held during the last two weeks of July. The ten-day extravaganza of delightful mid-summer madness is a revival of the gay '90s and of the 1898 gold rush. A Mardi Gras atmosphere pervades as residents and visitors join in parading bands, dancing in the streets, gambling in the Golden Garter Casino, horse racing, gold panning, street shows, midway rides, agricultural displays, waterskiing competitions, and boat races. Home-made rafts compete in the Sourdough Raft Race on the North Saskatchewan River, where plunging ashore to claim the garter off the leg of a dancing girl is a prerequisite of victory. The Whitewater Canoe Regatta from Rocky Mountain House to Edmonton is a three-day test of endurance, skill and nerve.

Buildings are transformed by false store fronts, bearing

the names of merchants and merchandise of a century past. Klondike-style costumes can be rented or purchased for the Sunday Promenade, when thousands of people, gaily dressed as dance hall girls, Apple Annies, flower girls, dapper gentlemen, hirsute prospectors, shoeshine boys, and Keystone Cops, cavort through the blocked off business section of downtown Edmonton. Strolling minstrels, honky tonk musicians and barbershop quartets entertain the crowds.

Other annual festivals include the Canadian Finals Rodeo in November, and Heritage Days, which takes place in August in Hawrelak Park and features three dozen ethnic displays representing various groups of Canadians.

Located 560 kilometers north of the American border, Edmonton lies at an altitude of 665 metres, and at a latitude of 53 degrees. The latitude accounts for the short winter days when the mercury may drop to a chilly -40° Celsius. Nevertheless, Edmonton enjoys more hours of sunshine annually than any other Canadian city. The Rocky Mountains to the west absorb moisture from Pacific winds, resulting in low precipitation and humidity. During the long sunny days of summer when the climate is kinder, temperatures average 25° Celsius.

But winter in Edmonton does not mean hibernation; people have adapted to their environment in other ways. In spite of, or perhaps because of, iron frosts, Edmontonians, with their ever-increasing incomes and cultural diversity have developed an enthusiastic interest in artistic and cultural activities.

Jubilee Auditorium is home to the Alberta Ballet, the Edmonton Symphony Orchestra, and the Edmonton Opera

Society. The opera company, which has featured such singers as Sills, Sutherland and Stratas, is one of the few opera companies in the world which is in the black, and is the only regional opera company ever used by the Canadian Broadcasting Company for a major production. Half a dozen live theatres are also flourishing. The most impressive is the Citadel, a magnificent glass and steel complex containing three theatres, a restaurant, a gallery in the lobby, and a theatre workshop. Assorted art galleries throughout the city are thriving as well.

The crisp clear dry air of winter inspires and invigorates hockey players, skaters, curlers, hikers, skiers and snowmobilers. Light rail transit connects downtown with the Coliseum, home of the National Hockey League Edmonton Oilers, and with the 45,000 seat Commonwealth Stadium, built for the Commonwealth Games which Edmonton hosted in the summer of 1978. The reigning Grey Cup champions, the Edmonton Eskimos of the Canadian Football League, now use Commonwealth Stadium during football season and play before a full house every game.

Amid the sleek skyscrapers downtown, an ever-expanding system of underground pedestrian concourses link all-weather shopping areas, office buildings, hotels, and the rapid transit system. Meanwhile an increasing number of high rise apartment and office buildings are fanning out towards sprawling suburbs of shopping centres and comfortable modern homes. The city is constantly annexing more lands, laying out more streets, and building more buildings.

The only Canadian city to have earned recognition as a "Green Survival City", Edmonton claims 50 percent more green space per capita than any other Canadian city. Recreational facilities include 176 hockey rinks, 17 curling rinks, 14 golf courses, 15 swimming centres, 12 public tennis centres and numerous picnic grounds. Within a radius of 160 kilometres, more than 50 lakes are available for recreational use.

The city is justly proud of its Capital City Recreation Park, North America's biggest central park, running 16 kilometres along the magnificent and meandering North Saskatchewan River valley from the Legislative Grounds to Hermitage Park. Four pedestrian footbridges crossing the river link 30 kilometres of bicycle and hiking trails. Snowshoeing, cross-country skiing, and snowmobiling are also popular, here where white-tailed deer, muskrat, beaver, snowshoe hare, and 123 species of birds make their homes.

Also situated in the river valley, just off the James Macdonald Bridge, is the Muttart Conservatory, designed by Edmonton architect Peter Hemingway. Three glass pyramid pavilions, each with its own environmental control including rain, house flora of tropical, arid and temperate climatic zones. A fourth pyramid contains seasonal ornamental displays of flowering plants, while the fifth pyramid and central core contains a sunken theatre for lectures and discussions.

The Queen Elizabeth Planetarium features armchair trips to distant galaxies. As gateway to the north, Edmonton is an appropriate home for the Canadian Aviation Hall of Fame, located east of the Civic Centre on Jasper Avenue. The Hall of Fame tells the story of Canada's aviation pioneers.

Displays at the Provincial Museum illustrate the natural and human history of the province.

In Fort Edmonton park, a reconstruction of the early trading post goes back in time to almost a century ago, with its boardwalk on 1885 Street, the horseyard, the servants' quarters at the John Rowand House, the Indian Trading Store and McDougall's General Store. Also in the park is the John Janzen Nature Centre which illustrates the geological eras preceding man's recorded history.

The Valley Zoo, where Mary's Little Lamb sleeps in the sun and where squirrels and chipmunks live in Noah's Ark, is a delightful combination of fantasy and reality for the young and the young at heart. The Northern Alberta Game Farm, approximately 24 kilometres north, contains Al Oeming's original collection of wildlife from all over the world, running free in natural settings. Elk, buffalo and the pygmy shrew roam as in days of yore in the Elk Island National Park, 36 kilometres east of Edmonton.

At Vegreville, 52 kilometres farther east, rests the world's largest "pysanka" or Easter egg, painted in colourful traditional Ukrainian patterns. In the 95th to 97th Streets area of Edmonton, there are several eastern churches and Ukrainian shops and museums. The Saturday morning Public Market on 97th Street is also worth a visit.

The University of Alberta, situated on the south bank of the North Saskatchewan River, was founded in 1908, with an initial enrolment of 45 students. Today there are nearly 20,000 full-time students enrolled in 16 different faculties. The Northern Alberta Institute of Technology, Canada's largest technical institute, offers 56 business, industrial and vocational programs.

For respite from a round of sightseeing, downtown Edmonton offers a variety of lounges and restaurants. Menu specialties range from Korean kimchee to Ukrainian perogies. LaRonde, the revolving bar and restaurant on the 24th floor of the Chateau LaCombe Hotel, features a superb panorama of the city and environs, or the "big sky country" as it is affectionately called. An observation deck on the 33rd floor tops the sleek new Alberta Government Telephone Tower, which, at 134 metres, is the tallest building in the city. Located just across from the historic chateau-style Macdonald Hotel, the tower dominates McCauley Plaza, named in honour of Edmonton's first mayor whose house and barn once occupied this site.

The people who have built and who inhabit this ultra-modern city have varied backgrounds. In recent years, immigrants have come from rural areas in the province, from other less industrialized provinces and from the United States and Europe. About 45 percent of the population is British in origin, 13 percent is Ukrainian, 12 percent is German, 7 percent is French, 5 percent is Scandinavian, with the rest having assorted ethnic origins.

Edmontonians are farmers, cultivating crops of wheat, barley, hay, rapeseed, flaxseed, sugar beets, rye, mustard and raising poultry, pigs and herds of fine sheep and cattle on the prairies surrounding the city. Edmontonians are also urbanites — oil millionaires, entrepreneurs, scientists, technologists and other business, professional and service people. They are predominantly young people; three-quarters of them are under 45 years of age.

But regardless of their age, their jobs or their ethnic origins, Edmontonians enjoy a reputation for warmth, friendliness and hospitality. Maybe it's because many of them still remember what it was like to be a newcomer. Whatever the reason, they seem to share a vibrant kindred pioneering spirit. And they have wooed the west and won.

Preceding page: The High Level Bridge, which opened in 1913, crosses the North Saskatchewan River in downtown Edmonton. Framed by the bridge is The Alberta Legislature.

Opposite: The Macdonald Hotel as seen from the bank of the North Saskatchewan River.

Top left: The Canadian National building is one of many sleek new downtown skyscrapers.

Below: Sunset over downtown.

Opposite: The interior of the ultra-modern Edmonton Centre. Situated close to the Art Gallery, Public Library, and the new Citadel Theatre, the centre offers climate-controlled shopping in over eighty stores.

Above: The Commonwealth Games Kinsman Aquatic Centre, built for the 1978 Commonwealth Games, contains more water than any other aquatic centre in North America and is the third largest one in the world.

Opposite page above: The main entrance to the Legislative Building, and to the right The Trader, a bronze by John Weaver. The Trader can be seen behind the Edmonton Public Library.

Opposite page below: The Law Courts, and to the left, futuristic art outside the Edmonton Art Gallery.

Above: The Legislative Building with its vaulted dome was built in Victorian-style architecture in 1912, on the site of the original Fort Edmonton.

Opposite: The rails in the Canadian National yards gleam golden in the afternoon sunshine.

Preceding pages: A brief summer storm toward day's end lends a pink glow to Jasper Avenue, Edmonton's main street.

Above: The 29 storey Canadian National Railway tower is an integral part of the Civic Centre complex.

Opposite: Entrance to the Light Rail Transit System.
Edmonton is the smallest city in the hemisphere to open
a subway system.

Above: A bird's-eye view of Commonwealth Stadium, built for
the Commonwealth Games which Edmonton hosted in the
summer of 1978.

Above and below: Refinery Row on Highway 16A east of Edmonton is a string of industrial chemical plants, gigantic storage tanks, and pipeline pumping stations.

Above and below: Refinery Row. Oil, sometimes called black gold, fuels the economy of Edmonton and Alberta. Edmonton refineries currently produce 60 percent of Canada's pretroleum products.

Right: Window boxes of colourful geraniums decorate one of Edmonton's older homes.

Below: Edmonton's concrete emporium stands like a sentinel guarding the great northwestern plain.

Opposite: The Alberta Government Telephone building reflects the amber light of sundown.

Opposite: The MacDonald Hotel, which dominated the sky line for many years, seems small when viewed with its newer neighbours.

Above: The Alberta Legislature in winter. The parliament buildings sit sedately on the north bank of the North Saskatchewan River.

Opposite: Klondike Days, held in late July each year,
revive the gaiety of the 1890s, with colourful costumes,
parades and other entertainment.

Above: Dancing girls, outfitted in turn-of-the-century
costumes complete with garters, entertain thousands
during Klondike Days.

Opposite: Flowers blossoming in summertime at William Hawrelak Park in the North Saskatchewan River valley.

Upper: The Hub Building, a student residence with shops and restaurants on the University of Alberta campus.

Lower: One of the older buildings at the University of Alberta, which was founded in 1908.

Preceding pages: Downtown Edmonton at dusk.

Right: The Northlands Race Track.

Below: The solitude of Cold Lake, 200 kilometres northeast of Edmonton on highway 28.

Opposite: Llama at the Northern Alberta Game Farm, which contains Al Oeming's original collection of wildlife from all over the world.

Above: The Soughdough Raft Races on the North Saskatchewan River. *Below:* The Citadel Theatre. This complex contains three theatres, restaurant, gallery, and theatre workshop.

Above: A Ukrainian Church. About 13 percent of Edmontonians are Ukrainian in origin.
Below: Winston Churchill Square.

Opposite page above: Natural Charm, an import boutique, and to the right, antique lamps from the Lawson Collection.

Above: A Ukrainian church near Wasel.

Opposite page below: The Queen Elizabeth Planetarium, Canada's first public planetarium when it was opened in 1960. At the right, a bicycle race on the Legislative grounds.

Opposite: Hot air balloons. Balloonists and spectators gather in Capital City Recreation Park on most weekends during the summer.

Left: Bronze statue outside the Provincial Museum.

Below: Edmonton from the air. The Legislative Building can be seen to the left.

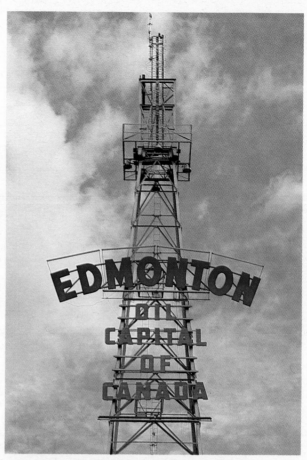

Opposite page above: Government House, the previous residence of Alberta's Lieutenant-Governor has been recently refurbished so that it may be used for official provincial gatherings. To the right, an oil derrick welcomes visitors to the city.

Above: During Klondike Days, fireworks displays shower the night with light.

Opposite page below: The Sunday promenade during Klondike Days, and office architecture in downtown Edmonton.

Above, below, and opposite page: Scenes from Fort Edmonton Park, an ambitious project now underway, covering 153 acres at the southern end of the Quesnel Bridge. The project when completed will reflect Edmonton's geological and cultural development. Planned are dioramas of geological ages, two Indian villages, a hangar commemorating the bush pilots who opened up the north, street scenes of the oil boom, and gold rush days.

Opposite: An oil rig, a familiar sight on the flatlands around Edmonton. Millions of years ago, dinosaurs roamed these prairies. These modern monsters stay in one place but produce great quantities of oil, and more of them keep appearing regularly.

Above: An old barn on highway # 2. Agriculture is Alberta's original prime industry.

Following page: The pyramid pavilions of the Muttart Conservatory. Flora of tropical, arid and temperate climatic zones can be seen inside.

Opposite: Lawn bowling on the manicured grounds of The Alberta Legislature.

Above: Both downhill and cross-country skiing are popular winter pastimes in Capital City Recreation Park, North America's biggest central park.

Opposite: The Principal Plaza, Jasper Avenue's newest skyscraper, is scheduled for completion in June, 1980. The exterior is being finished in mirrored glass and aluminum sheeting.

Above: Signs for all occasions on a downtown street. In this case the street is 82nd Avenue.

Opposite: The red glow of a prairie sunset.

Above: A multiple exposure of neon at night
suggests a variety of evening entertainments.

Titles Available in this series:—
**Vancouver, Manitoba, Victoria,
British Columbia, The Yukon,
Toronto, Edmonton, Calgary,
British Columbia: The Pacific Province.**

In preparation:—
**Canada, Vancouver Island, Saskatchewan,
The Fraser Valley, The Okanagan Valley,
The Mountains of British Columbia.**

Whitecap Books Limited
1615 Venables Street,
Vancouver, B.C. V5L 2H1
(604) 251-3616